GW00707892

The Essential

DESMOND TUTU

compiled by John Allen

MAYIBUYE BOOKS
University of the Western Cape, Bellville

DAVID PHILIP PUBLISHERS
Cape Town

First published 1997 in southern Africa by David Philip
Publishers (Pty) Ltd, 208 Werdmuller Centre, Claremont
7700 and Mayibuye Books, University of the Western
Cape, Private Bag X17, Bellville 7535

ISBN 0-86486-346-2

Mayibuye History and Literature Series No. 85

Printed in South Africa by National Book Printers,
Drukkery Street, Goodwood, Western Cape

CONTENTS

FAITH AND LIFE

Ubuntu

You know the story of Adam and Eve. Adam lived in a garden and he was happy. In the garden everything was just lovely. The animals loved each other and they were friendly. The lion played with the lamb. There was no fighting, there was no bloodshed. They were all vegetarians in the garden. Did we say everything was all right in the garden? No, not quite, because God – who was friendly with Adam and used to visit him – said, 'It is not good for man to be alone.' So God asked Adam to choose a mate from the animals passing in procession before him.

'What about this one?' God asks.

'Nope,' says Adam.

'Well, how about this one?'

'Aikona!'

'And this one?'

'Not on your life.'

And so God put Adam to sleep, took his rib and formed that lovely, delectable creature, Eve. When Adam awoke and saw Eve, he said 'Wow! This is just what the doctor ordered!'

That story speaks about how human beings need each other, that God has made us so that we know we need each other.

In our African idiom we say: 'A person is a person through other persons.' None of us comes into the world fully formed. We would not know how to think, or walk, or speak, or behave as human beings unless we learned it from other human beings. We need other human beings in order to be human. The solitary, isolated human being is really a contradiction in terms.

St Paul says we in the church are like a body, and a body is a body because it has different organs performing different functions. I have a very big nose. Imagine if your body, as St Paul says, was all nose. How would I be able to walk? How would I be able to see? How would I be able to speak? So St Paul tells us this wonderful thing about us, that we belong together.

God is smart. God does not make us too self-sufficient, so that we should realise we need one another. We have our own gifts and that makes us unique, but I have gifts that you do not have and you have gifts that I do not have. The totally self-sufficient person, if ever there could be one, is subhuman.

The first law of our being is that we are set in a delicate network of interdependence with our fellow human beings and with the rest of God's creation. We are meant to live as sisters and brothers, as members of one family, the human family, God's family. We are created for peace, for harmony, for togetherness. All kinds of things go horribly, badly wrong when we flout that fundamental law, when some spend billions on instruments of death and destruction. We know it is an obscenity, for even a small fraction of the budgets of death would ensure that God's children everywhere had enough to eat, had a decent and stable family life, adequate housing, clothing and education, and a clean supply of water.

⚹

The West has achieved a great deal through individual initiative and ingenuity and must be commended for these often spectacular achievements. But the cost may have been high. All this has permitted a culture of achievement and success to evolve, assiduously encouraging the rat-race mentality. The awful consequence is that persons tend then not to be valued in and for themselves with a worth that is intrinsic.

In Africa we have something called *ubuntu* in Nguni languages, or *botho* in Sotho, which is difficult to translate into English. It is the essence of being human. It speaks of the fact that my humanity is caught up and is inextricably bound up in yours. I am human because I belong. It speaks about wholeness, it speaks about compassion. A person with *ubuntu* is welcoming, hospitable, warm and generous, willing to share. Such people are open and available to others, affirming of others, does not feel threatened that others are able and good, for they have a proper self-assurance that comes from knowing that they belong in a greater whole and are diminished when others are humiliated or diminished, when others are tortured or oppressed, or treated as if they were less than who they are. It gives people resilience, enabling them to survive and emerge still human

7

despite all efforts to dehumanise them. It means it is not a great good to be successful through being aggressively competitive, that our purpose is social and communal harmony and well-being.

Created in the image of God

What the Christian faith says is that every single person – whether you are tall or short, whether you are a Studebaker or a spring chicken, whether you are rich or poor, whatever your circumstances – you are created in the image of God.

The church goes on to teach, following St Paul, that we are temples, sanctuaries of the Holy Spirit, that we are God-carriers. Human beings must not just by rights be respected, but they must be held in awe and reverence. If we took our theology seriously, we should not just greet each other. We should really genuflect before one another. Buddhists are more correct, since they bow profoundly as they greet one another, saying the God in me acknowledges the God in you.

Each human being is of intrinsic worth because each human being is created in the image of God. That is an incredible, a staggering assertion about human beings. It might seem to be an innocuous religious truth, until you say it in a situation of injustice and oppression and exploitation. When I was rector of a small parish in Soweto, I would tell an old lady whose white employer called her

'Annie' because her name was too difficult: 'Mama, as you walk the dusty streets of Soweto and they ask who you are, you can say, "I am God's partner, God's representative, God's viceroy – that's who I am."'

To treat a child of God as if he or she was less than this is not just wrong, which it is; is not just evil, as it often it is; not just painful, as it often must be for the victim: it is veritably blasphemous, for it is to spit in the face of God. It is because God has said this about each one of us, that our faith in God demands the obedience of our whole being in opposing injustice. For not to oppose injustice is to disobey God.

To oppose injustice and oppression is not something that is merely political. No, it is profoundly religious. Can you imagine what the Gospel means to people whose dignity is trodden underfoot every day of their life, to those who have had their noses rubbed in the dust as if they didn't count? Can you think of anything more subversive of a situation of injustice and oppression? Why should you need Marxist ideology or whatever? The Bible is dynamite in such a situation. In South Africa, when they banned books, we told the government the book they should have banned long ago was the Bible, for nothing could be more radical, more revolutionary, as we faced up to the awfulness of injustice, oppression and racism.

There is no neutrality in a situation of injustice and oppression. If you say you are neutral, you are a liar, for you have already taken sides with the powerful.

In the Christian point of view our God is one who took our human nature. Our God said, Inasmuch as you have done it to the least of these, my brethren and my sisters, you have done it to me. You don't have to go around looking for God. You don't have to say, Where is God? Turn round, the person on your right, the person on your left, the person behind you, the person in front of you, that is God.

God made us for freedom

God created us freely, for freedom. To be human in the understanding of the Bible is to be free to choose, free to choose to love or not to love, free to choose to obey or not to obey, free to be responsible or to shirk one's responsibility. To be human is to be a morally responsible creature, and moral responsibility is a nonsense when the person is in fact not free to choose from several available options. That is how God created us. It is part of being created in the image of God, this freedom which can make us into glorious creatures or damn us into hellish ones. God took an incredible risk in creating us human beings. God, who alone has the perfect right to be a totalitarian, has such a profound respect, nay reverence, for this freedom which he bestowed on us that he had much rather see us go freely to hell than compel us to go to heaven. As they say, hell is the greatest compliment God has paid us.

Our freedom does not come from any human being, our

freedom comes from God. This is what we mean when we say it is an inalienable right. This freedom is so much a part of the human make-up that it is not too far-fetched to say that an unfree human being is in a sense a contradiction in terms. The ideal society is one in which its members enjoy their freedom to be human freely, provided they do not thereby infringe the freedom of others unduly. We are made to have freedom of association, of expression, of movement, the freedom to choose who will rule over us and how. We are made for this. It is ineluctable. It cannot ultimately be eradicated, this yearning for freedom to be human. This is what tyrants and unjust rulers have to contend with. They cannot in the end stop their victims from being human. They must come a cropper because they seek to deny something that cannot be denied. No matter how long and how repressive their unjust and undemocratic rule turns out to be, the urge for freedom remains as a subversive element threatening the overthrow of rigid repression. The tyrant is on a road to nowhere even though he may survive for an unconscionably long time and even though he may turn his country into a huge prison, riddled with informers. This may go on for too long in the view of the victims but the end cannot be in doubt. Freedom will break out. People are made for it just as plants tend towards the light and towards water.

Our God takes sides

God wanted his people, the children of Israel, to be freed

from bondage in Egypt. He could have done it on his own, but he wanted a human partner. So he went to Moses.

'Hi, Moses.'

'Hi, God.'

'I want you to go to the Pharaoh and tell him: "Let my people go."'

Moses was thoroughly flabbergasted: 'What? Me? What have I done now? Go to Pharaoh? Please, God, no! You can't be serious!'

Forgetting that God knew everything, Moses pleaded: 'God, you know I stammer. How can I address Pharaoh?'

Mercifully, God did not accept Moses' first negative reactions. If he had, in a real sense the children of Israel would still be in Egypt in bondage. The God we worship is the Exodus God, the great liberator God who leads us out of all kinds of bondage.

Do you remember when God spoke to Moses? He said, 'I have seen the suffering of my people. I have heard their cry. I know their suffering and am come down to deliver them.' Our God is a God who knows. Our God is a God who sees. Our God is a God who hears. Our God is a God who comes down to deliver.

Why does Jesus Christ sit at table with harlots and sinners and tax collectors, a thoroughly disreputable lot? Because in his society they were rejected. The Jesus in whom I believe demonstrated the bias of God in favour of those who are the despised, the powerless, the marginalised, those without clout. They had a special place in his Father's heart. He demonstrated his solidarity with them by the manner of his birth – in a stable, not in a royal palace, of parents who did not even have the kind of influence to make an innkeeper find them a room in a full hotel.

Our God is not a neutral God. We have a God who does take sides. Our God is a God who has a bias for the weak, and we, who are the people of this God, who have to reflect the character of this God, have no option but to have a like special concern for those who are pushed to the edges of society, for those who because they are different seem to be without a voice. The church must speak up on their behalf, on behalf of the drug addicts and the down-and-outs, on behalf of the poor, the hungry, the marginalised ones, on behalf of those who because they are different dress differently, on behalf of those who because they have different sexual orientations from our own tend to be pushed away to the periphery. The church of God must be where our Lord and Saviour, Jesus, would be, this one who was vilified for being the friend of sinners.

Would you say Moses was a religious leader or a political leader? Was God acting religiously or politically when he set free a slave people? Throughout the Bible you will see how frequently the prophets act on behalf of God or speak on behalf of God and they speak in what we call political areas.

What is also interesting is how many times the prophets say

that if your religion does not affect the way you live your life, it is a religion that God rejects. Isaiah says a fast where you deny yourself food but which does not relate to how you treat your neighbours is rejected by God. He says the fast that he wants is that you loose the fetters of injustice and set free those who have been crushed, that you share your food with the hungry, take the homeless poor into your house and clothe the naked. The prophet speaks about God's Holy Spirit anointing the one whom God sends to preach the Good News, to set at liberty all of those who are oppressed. And Jesus Christ accepts this as a description of his programme. Now, of course, setting people free is not just setting them free politically, it is setting them free from all that enslaves them, and sin is the greatest enslaver. Then in the parable of the last judgment, Jesus says God is not going to judge us by whether we went to church or prayed: this is not to say they are not important; but if we go to church, if we pray, then it ought to show in how we act. When you meet a hungry person, you feed him; someone who is thirsty, you give him drink; one who is naked, you give him something to clothe himself; because if you do this you are doing it really to Jesus Christ himself.

⁂

Our religion is not what Marx castigated as the opiate of the people. A church that tries to pacify us, telling us not to concentrate on the things of this world but of the other, the next world, needs to be treated with withering scorn and contempt as being not only wholly irrelevant but actually blasphemous. It deals with pie in the sky when you die –

and I am not interested, nobody is interested, in post-mortem pies. We want our pies here and now.

God with us

Do you remember the wonderful story in the Book of Daniel about the time God's people were being persecuted by the king who expected them to bow down before a graven image? The king set up a golden statue and said that anyone who refused to worship it was going to become a Kentucky Fried Chicken, because he was going to be thrown into the fiery furnace. Now Shadrach, Meshach and Abednego refused to obey the royal decree. The king called the three and tried to be nice to them: 'I know there are people who mislead you. You will worship the image.' They said: 'What? No, man.' So the king said: 'Do you know who I am? I am the king here, I am in charge. We are going to stoke up the fire seven times hotter than it ever was, because you don't listen to me.'

The story says the fire was so hot it burned to death the soldiers who carried the three to the furnace. But as the king looked into the fire, thinking they were *kant en klaar*, he could not believe his eyes. For they were walking in the fire! No, there were not three! There was a fourth with them, and the king looked and said: 'There is a fourth who looks like a god.'

The God we worship is not one who gives good advice from a safe distance. He doesn't tell his people to wear asbestos suits before going into the furnace. He goes right

15

in there with them.

❧

A Nazi guard was taunting his Jewish prisoner, who had been given the most filthy job, cleaning out the toilets. The guard was standing above him, looking down at him, and said: 'Where is your God now?' The prisoner replied: 'Right here with me in the muck.'

Racism

Racism declares that what invests people with value is something extrinsic, a biological attribute arbitrarily chosen, something which in the nature of the case only a few people can have, making them instantly an elite, a privileged group not because of merit or effort but because of an accident of birth. In South Africa they said the thing which gave you value was the colour of your skin; you were white and therefore you had value.

❧

Suppose we did not use skin colour to mark what gave people their imagined racial superiority. Since I have a large nose, suppose we said privilege was to be reserved for people with large noses only, and those many millions with small noses were to be excluded.

In South Africa they used to have signs on toilets saying 'Whites Only'. Suppose you are looking for a toilet and instead it says 'Large Noses Only'. If you have a small nose, you are in trouble if nature is calling. We also used to have universities in South Africa reserved for whites. The primary entry qualification was not academic ability but a biological irrelevance. Let's say it changed and the quality that determined whether you could enter was size of nose – if you had a small nose and you wanted to attend the university for large noses only, then you would have to apply to the Minister of Small Nose Affairs for permission to attend the Large Nose University. Absolutely and utterly ridiculous.

What does the colour of one's skin tell us that is of any significance about a person? Nothing, of course, absolutely nothing. It does not say whether the person is warm-hearted or kind, clever and witty, or whether that person is good.

They say that when God created human beings, he made them out of dust. Then he put the first lot into an oven, just as you fire bricks in a kiln. For some reason God became engaged in other things and forgot that he had put this lot in the oven. When he remembered and rushed to open it, they were burnt to cinders. They say that is how black people came about. Then God put in the second lot. This time God was over-anxious and opened the oven too quickly. This lot was underdone, and these were the white people. That story tells a profound truth, a truth asserted by all faiths, that human beings have an intrinsic worth that does not depend on extraneous things such as skin colour, ethnicity or whatever.

Jesus Christ has broken down the middle wall of partition, that wall which used to separate the Jew from the Gentile, making them enemies. That wall has now been broken down, and in Jesus Christ we are all one. There is now no longer Jew nor Gentile, male nor female, free nor slave, we are all one in our Lord and Saviour, Jesus Christ.

There is an old film entitled *The Defiant Ones* which depicts two escaped convicts manacled together. One is black and the other white. They fall into a ditch with steep, slippery sides. One convict claws his way nearly to the top and just as he is about to make it, he discovers that he can't get out because he is still manacled to his mate at the bottom, so he slithers back down. The only way they can make it out of that ditch is together – up, and up, and up, then out together. In South Africa we can survive only together, black and white. We can be truly free, ultimately, only together, black and white. We can be human only together, black and white.

Grace

The prophet Jeremiah was a retiring, sensitive soul who recoiled at the demanding vocation of having to address a recalcitrant and stubborn people about their persistent disobedience and warn them of impending divine retribution and punishment. God had to reassure him, so we have the delightful account of the call of Jeremiah where God utters the startling words: 'Before I formed you in the womb, I knew you.' We might say today that God didn't know much about human biology, but what God wanted Jeremiah to know was that it was not as if he had said, 'Wow, these Israelites are in a real pickle. What am I going to do about it? Ah, I know what I will do – I will appoint Jeremiah as prophet.' No, God was declaring to Jeremiah that long before he was an idea in his father's or mother's head, God knew him. He was no divine afterthought. He was part of the divine plan from all eternity. He was no accident. None of us is a divine afterthought. I sometimes say some of us might look like accidents, but no one is an accident. God has chosen us from all eternity to be an indispensable part of his divine plan.

The Old Testament did not teach a religion of achievement, of personal effort. No, at its best it taught a religion of grace, that it was all due to the generosity of God and that our salvation was a matter of divine gift. In Exodus, God had already delivered his people, had already acted on their behalf, long before they could have done anything to deserve it. They were just a rabble of slaves when God chose them. They were not a particularly impressive lot – anything but. The Bible is quite scathing about them, depicting them as thoroughly impossible and quite undeserving of the divine choice. But that is precisely the point. They were chosen not because they deserved it, not because they worked hard to achieve. No, their choice was pure grace. It was pure gift. The initiative was not theirs but God's.

Note that the Exodus, the crossing of the Red Sea, the act of divine grace came first, and then the giving of the law, the Ten Commandments, at Sinai. This sequence is quite crucial, demonstrating that the religion advocated in the Old Testament was a religion of grace. It was not a religion of performance in which the adherents had to impress God so that God would then accept them, would then have to love them as a reward for their goodness, for their achievement. The law was given not so that, through their observance of it, the people would impress God, who would then reward them by the deliverance of the Exodus. No, the law was given as a vehicle for expressing their gratitude for what God had already done.

In the New Testament, in Ephesians, we are told that God chose us to be his children in Jesus Christ *before the foundation of the world*. Do you realise that this refers to you, to me, to each one of us? Before the foundation of the world, before we were conceived, God had already decided he wanted us. Long before we could have done anything to earn it, to deserve it, God freely, graciously, chose you, chose me, chose each one of us to be his children. It could not depend on whether we were good. It could not depend on our ability to impress God, on our success. That is the Good News: that God loved us, that God loves us and that God will love us for ever unchangingly. You don't need to do anything at all because God loves you already long before you could do anything to impress him.

Jesus tried to proclaim this Gospel by word and deed. He associated with the scum of society, who had no claim on him and who knew that they had no claim on him on the basis of their goodness. They knew they could be saved only by an unbelievable act of divine mercy and love, and they were ready therefore to throw themselves on that mercy and had the right attitude of openness and receptivity. And Jesus taught that he had come to seek and to find not the righteous but the lost and the sinners. He scandalised the prim and proper people of his day who believed that he was lowering standards horribly badly. Now anyone could enter heaven.

In most of our images of the Good Shepherd, the lost sheep is shown as a lovely fluffy little lamb being held by Jesus, who stands there looking as if a soup plate is suspended over his head. I recall a memorable sermon by Professor Denis Nineham when I was at King's College, London. He drew our attention to an insight by showing that these pictures distort our understanding of the parable. The point of the story becomes clear when we realise that fluffy little lambs very rarely stray from their mummies. The sheep that will stray is that obstreperous old ram which won't have nice cuddly fleece. It will have torn its fleece on a fence, perhaps, and fallen into a ditch of dirty, stinking water. It will smell to high heaven. That's the one the Good Shepherd goes after, leaving ninety-nine perfectly well-behaved sheep in the wilderness. When he finds this rogue, this utterly troublesome one, this is the one he will lift onto his shoulders and bring back home rejoicing, saying, 'Hey, let's have a party because I found the one that was lost.'

If Jesus had waited until we were die-able for, then he would have waited until the cows came home.

God loves you not because you are good. No, God loves you, period. You may become good because God loves you. Your goodness is a consequence of, a response to, God's love.

God loves us not because we are lovable. No, we are lovable precisely because God loves us.

I'm usually in enough trouble as it is without getting into more trouble with the things I say in church, but in a sense it actually doesn't matter what we do. For nothing we can do, no matter how bad, will change God's love for us. But in another way it does matter, because when you are in love you want to please the one you love. Only those who have not been in love don't know how demanding love can be – more demanding than the law.

Friends, we have turned Christianity, a religion of grace, into a religion of virtue, of achievement, of works. Ours is a culture of achievement and success. We carry over these attitudes to our relationship with God. We work ourselves to a frazzle trying to impress God, to earn God's approval and acceptance. We cannot believe that our relationship with God, our standing before God, has got nothing to do with our performance, our works.

Someone has said: 'There is nothing you can do to make God love you more, for God already loves you perfectly and totally.' But more wonderfully, there is nothing you can do to make God love you less – absolutely nothing, for God already loves you and will love you for ever.

⁂

Do you know how precious you are to God? In the sight of God, you are as if you were the only human being. You are so precious to God that the very hairs of your head are numbered, and Scripture says your name is engraved on the palms of God's hands. 'Can a mother', God asks, 'forget the child she bore?' That is a most unlikely thing, quite unnatural, but it could happen. God says, even if that most unlikely thing were to happen, God's love wouldn't allow him to forget you or me. When God created us out of dust, God breathed the breath of God into our nostrils. We are precious things that God carries gently. God carries each one of us as if we were fragile, and if God dropped us, we would be smashed into smithereens.

God's partners

When, according to the Christian faith, we had fallen into the clutches of the devil and were enslaved by sin, God chose Mary, a teenager in a small village, to be the mother of his Son. He sent an archangel to visit her.

Knock, knock.

'Come in.'

'Er, Mary?'

'Hello.'

'Mary, God would like you to be the mother of his son.'

'What? Me!! In this village you can't even scratch your-self without everybody knowing about it! You want me to be an unmarried mother? I'm a decent girl, you know. Sorry, try next door.'

If she had said that, we would have been up a creek. Mercifully, marvellously, Mary said, 'Behold the handmaid of the Lord; be it unto me according to thy word,' and the universe breathed a cosmic sigh of relief, because she made it possible for the Saviour of the world to be born.

—

When there is someone hungry, God wants to perform the miracle of feeding that person. But it won't any longer be through manna falling from heaven. Normally, more usual-ly, God can do nothing until we provide God with the means, the bread and the fish, to feed the hungry. When a person is naked, God would want to perform the miracle of clothing that person, but it won't be with a Carducci suit or Calvin Klein outfit floating from heaven. No, it will be because you, and you, and all of us have agreed to be God's fellow workers, providing God with the raw material for performing miracles.

—

There is a church in Rome with a statue of a Christ without arms. When you ask why, you are told that it shows how God relies on us, his human partners, to do his work for him. Without us, God has no eyes; without us, God has no ears; without us, God has no arms. He waits upon us, and relies on us. Won't you be God's partner in the world?

~

The individual is the indispensable agent of change. You should not be daunted by the magnitude of the task before you. Your contribution can inspire others, embolden others who are timid, to stand up for the truth in the midst of a welter of distortion, propaganda and deceit; stand up for human rights where these are being violated with impunity; stand up for justice, freedom and love where they are trampled underfoot by injustice, oppression, hatred and harsh cruelty; stand up for human dignity and decency at a time when these are in desperately short supply.

~

God calls on us to be his partners to work for a new kind of society where people count; where people matter more than things, more than profits; where human life is not just respected but positively revered; where people will be secure and not suffer from the fear of hunger, from ignorance, from disease; where there will be more gentleness, more caring, more sharing, more compassion, more laughter, where there is peace and not war.

~

In our best moments and deep inside us, we know that goodness and righteousness and courage are admirable attributes which we crave. Isn't it fascinating that we may envy and even respect the hard, successful businessperson, but we are seldom moved to love them or admire them? Yet what happens when the world is confronted by a Mahatma

Gandhi, a Mother Teresa, a Helder Camara, a Martin Luther King Jr., a Nelson Mandela, an Oscar Romero. We thrill, we admire them, we even get to adore and love them. People recognise goodness and they want to emulate it. The good people are hardly ever successful as the world computes success. Often they are failures, for they tend to be arrested, tortured and even killed. Now the Bible seems crazy to suggest that somehow when we lose our lives, paradoxically we gain them. That seems to be a recipe for abject failure. But is it?

Authentic spirituality

The Bible and our faith and its tradition declare unequivocally that for an authentic Christian existence the absolute priority must be spirituality. When we want to grow in our intimacy with God, through prayer, Bible reading, meditation, retreats and regular use of the sacraments, then we must be growing in contemplation of the God who has created us for the divine life. A church that does not pray is quite useless. Christians who do not pray are of no earthly worth.

It is dangerous to pray, for an authentic spirituality is subversive of injustice. Oppressive and unjust governments should stop people praying to the Christian God, should stop them reading and meditating on the Bible, for these activities will constrain them to work for the establishment of God's Kingdom of justice, of peace, of laughter, of joy, of caring, of sharing, of reconciliation, of compassion. These activities will not permit us to luxuriate in a spiritual ghetto, insulated against the harsh realities of life out there as most of God's children experience it.

The Spirit of God sends us into the fray, as it sent our Lord, but we must observe the sequence in his life and we will see that disengagement, waiting on God, always precedes engagement. He waited to be anointed with God's Spirit ,which made him preach the Good News to the poor and the setting free of captives. He went into retreat in the wilderness. He had experience of the transfiguration and then went into the valley of human need and crass misunderstanding and insistent demand. If it was so vital for the Son of God, it can't be otherwise for his followers. Spirituality is really all we can give the world that is distinctive. The only resources we possess are ultimately spiritual resources.

Transfiguration

I doubt that we could produce a more spectacular example of transfiguration than what God did with the Cross. Most people would have been filled with revulsion had someone gone and got an electric chair or a gallows or the guillotine and set it up as an object of reverence. Anyone who tried to do that would have been condemned out of court as morbid with a macabre and ghoulish sense of humour. Well, look at the Cross. This was a ghastly instrument of death, of an excruciatingly awful death reserved for the most notorious malefactors. It was an object of dread and shame and yet what a turn-around has happened.

This thing, which was an object of shame, death and destruction, Christians wear with pride, use to adorn their most sacred places; they sign themselves with it at solemn moments in their lives and they hope it will be traced over them when they breathe their last. This instrument of a horrendous death has been spectacularly transfigured. From being a means of death, it is now perceived to be the source of life eternal. Far from being an object of vilification and shame, it is an object of veneration.

Africans apprehending God

Africans apprehend God and the things of God as Africans and have to express that experience of the divine in African ways. The impression has sometimes been given that you had to be, as it were, circumcised into a Westerner, if you were an African, before God could hear you. God couldn't hear you if you spoke an African language, you had to speak English, and God wouldn't recognise you unless you were wearing Western clothes. Africans ought not to be ashamed of being African. The trouble is that most Europeans forget that things like Easter eggs and Christmas trees are symbols from a pagan background which have been taken over and used as a means of communicating the Gospel. We can express our faith through symbols from our own culture. We don't have to protect God; we don't have to be scared on God's behalf. The truth of God is powerful.

Using the Bible

The Bible is not something that came dropping from heaven, written by the hand of God. It was written by human beings, so it uses human idiom and is influenced by the context in which whatever story was written. People need to be very careful. We tend to have literalists, people who believe in the verbal inerrancy of the Bible, who speak as if God dictated the Bible, whereas God used human beings as they were, and they spoke only as they could speak at that time. There are parts of the Bible that have no permanent worth – that is nothing to be sorry about, it is just to say that it is the Word of God in the words of men and women.

We make ghastly mistakes if we do not ask what genre a particular piece of literature is, because if we do not know its type then we are apt to pose inappropriate questions and will be frustrated in not getting the answers which we demand and which the particular literary material was never designed to provide. When you want to bake a cake you don't go to a geometry textbook for instructions.

The Bible did not intend to tell the how, but much more the why and by whom of creation. Those first chapters are much more like poetry than prose, replete with religious and not scientific truths, conveying profound truths about us, about God and about the universe we inhabit.

I am four-square in the Catholic faith that is enshrined in our prayer books, in our formularies, in the creeds. But when we say Jesus Christ ascended into heaven, you don't believe that he got into a kind of ecclesiastical lift that took him into the stratosphere. This is language that is being used figuratively because the realities that are being described are not human realities, they are supranatural realities. When we speak even about the resurrection of Jesus Christ, it is not the revivification of a corpse. It is speaking about a tremendous reality, that Jesus Christ is risen, his life is real, he is accessible to me here in South Africa, as he is accessible to someone in Timbuktu; that Jesus Christ is someone whose life makes a difference to me 2 000 years after he lived.

MEN AND WOMEN

My wife, Leah, has a car sticker which says, 'A woman who wants to be like a man has no ambition.'

❦

Leah once gave me a card for my birthday. The outside showed a lovely Darby and Joan couple, and said: 'We have a beautiful and unique relationship.' Which was very nice. Inside it said: 'I am beautiful, and you are certainly unique.'

❦

Theologically, biblically, socially, ecumenically, it is right to ordain women to the priesthood. The most radical act that can happen to any human being is to become a member of the body of Christ. If gender cannot be a bar to baptism, which makes us all representatives of Christ and partakers of the only priesthood there is, his royal priesthood, then gender cannot be a bar to ordination.

❦

The Bible is quite clear that the divine image is constitutive of humanity irrespective of gender. I cannot be opposed to racism, in which people are discriminated against as a result of something about which they can do nothing – their skin colour – and then accept with equanimity the gross injustice of penalising others for something else they can do nothing about – their gender.

❦

I gather that in heaven there were two queues. The notice above one said, 'Henpecked husbands,' and the second read, 'Husbands not henpecked.' The first queue was much the longer, while there was only one man in the second. St Peter asked him, 'What are you doing here?' The man said: 'Well, I don't know, my wife said I should come here.'

A lady went with her son to her husband's funeral. During the service the minister said so many nice things about her late husband that she turned to her son and whispered: 'I think we've come to the wrong funeral.'

One day Adam went off on his own and returned home very late. As far as Eve knew, they were the only two people in the garden. But just in case, she waited until Adam was asleep and then she counted his ribs.

Until women are deeply involved in opposing the violence in our country, we are not going to bring it to an end. All women must say, 'We have had enough of this, you men. We've had enough of this business. If you keep going out to fight and kill, we're not going to cook for you; we're not going to share your beds.'

APARTHEID SOUTH AFRICA

A South African was going to make his first parachute jump. He was told, 'It's quite easy, jump out of the plane, pull on this tog and the parachute will open. In the highly unlikely event that it doesn't, don't worry, just pull this second tog. It is absolutely certain, foolproof, that it will then open.' He made his jump and pulled the first tog. Nothing happened. He pulled the second. Nothing happened. As he was hurtling down, just before he hit the ground, someone shot past him in the opposite direction. He hollered: 'Help! Do you know anything about parachutes?' The other person shouted back: 'No! Do you know anything about pressure cookers?'

There is a story that when the missionaries came to Africa they had the Bible and black people had the land. They taught us to pray with our eyes shut, which we dutifully did. When we opened our eyes, we had the Bible and the missionaries had the land.

In the first stage, apartheid was blatantly and unashamedly racist. When the Nationalists won the 1948 elections, they embarked on a policy of putting the 'kaffir' in his place as the necessary corollary of white baasskap. Those were the days when they didn't care what the world thought and went around stampeding voters at election time by evoking the swart gevaar, showing whites a picture of an unkempt black man and saying, 'Would you like your daughter to marry this man.' These days, they say blacks have a retort: 'Show us your daughter first.'

They used to call us 'Natives' with a capital *N*, and years ago there used to be notices reading 'Natives and dogs not allowed.' The signs spoke eloquently about the attitude of some whites towards blacks. We were thought to be human but not quite as human as white people, for we lacked what seemed indispensable to that humanity, a particular skin colour.

There used to be road signs reading, 'Drive Carefully: Natives Cross Here.' Some wag changed one sign to read, somewhat hair-raisingly, 'Drive Carefully: Natives Very Cross Here.'

I remember going into a shop with my father when I was young. A slip of a girl, because she was white, could call my father 'boy' and there was nothing he could do about it. I would often be fuming inside just to see how he had been humiliated.

When we walked about in London, if we saw a policeman we would cross the road to ask him the way, even if we knew where we were going, just for the pleasure of being called 'Sir' and 'Madam'. In South Africa we would have been asked for our passes and run the risk of getting arrested.

The intention of Bantu Education was to teach '*Bantu*' children just enough English and Afrikaans so that they could understand instructions given by their white masters or mistresses. It was education for perpetual servanthood, indeed serfdom. It was designed to spawn unthinking, uncritical, docile zombies who would be the proverbial drawers of water and hewers of wood for their white overlords.

I am about to publish a dictionary to help people who are not too knowledgeable about the strange use of language that is characteristic of our country. If you heard someone say, we have a law called the Extension of University Education Act, you would assume, given the dictionary meaning of the words, that they were saying university education would now be made more readily and widely available than formerly. That would be so everywhere else in the world. Not in South Africa. That law was enacted to stop so-called open universities from admitting students of all races, and ethnic-based universities became the order of the day.

When the South African government was using its divide-and-rule tactics, classifying us on the basis of ethnicity, I told an audience in one of my addresses that my father was a Xhosa and my mother was a Tswana. When I asked what that made me, Harry Belafonte called out from the back: 'A Zulu!'

I am writing to you, Sir, because I have a growing nightmarish fear that unless something drastic is done very soon, then bloodshed and violence are going to happen in South African almost inevitably.

Letter to B.J. Vorster six weeks before the 1976 Soweto uprising

~

Even if we were to have a drastic amelioration of the situation of blacks, that would not be satisfactory because it would still be in the nature of concessions at the whim of those who have political power. What we want is not crumbs of concessions thrown from the master's table at his whim. We want to be at that table deciding the menu together, and that means universal suffrage. This was what whites told us was the meaning of democracy: government of the people, by the people, for the people – all the people, black and white, genuine majority rule.

~

All that black South Africans want is to be able to live as human beings created in the image of God and, therefore, of inestimable worth in the land of their birth, where their dignity as human beings is acknowledged and respected. Blacks don't want to drive white people into the sea. They just want a place in the sun in a land where all South Africans will be South Africans. That is a tautology, but an important tautology, for a citizen, by definition, shares in political decision-making through the franchise.

~

You could become an instant expert on South Africa by repeating a generalisation with the validity of a Euclidean theorem. It is this: what pleases most whites will almost certainly displease most blacks, and *vice versa*. I remember the story of a little boy who excitedly pointed to a flight of geese and said, 'Mommy, look, look at those gooses.' Mommy said, 'No darling, those are not gooses. We call them geese.' Little darling, nothing daunted, retorted, 'Well, they still look like gooses to me.'

It would be fair to say that everybody in South Africa was taken aback (some pleasantly and others rudely shaken) at the first utterances of P.W. Botha soon after he became Prime Minister. We couldn't quite believe our ears – had we heard correctly? Did he really say that whites would have to adapt or die? Had he really dismissed several of the Afrikaners' sacred cows?

Those were heady days ... Now things have changed, very sadly. Apart from the labour dispensation (much like the curate's egg, good in parts), we have not had much else in translating the rhetoric of reform into tangible and concrete reality. If anything, we see a veritable retreat on nearly all fronts.

Apartheid, we have been told by Dr Koornhof, is dead. Sadly we have not been invited to the funeral, nor seen the corpse.

Most whites believe we are in the throes of rapid change in our land and that leaves them all rather breathless. Looking at all this much-vaunted orgy of change, blacks tend to dismiss it as peripheral to their major concerns or as being merely cosmetic, and that really gets many whites hot under the collar.

In South Africa, the majority of the people, 80 per cent, are oppressed and downtrodden by a small minority. This minority controls all political power. I am an Archbishop in the church of God. In the land of my birth I do not vote because I cannot vote. An 18-year-old, because he or she is white, and more recently coloured and Indian, they can vote.

We have a land in which the vast majority have been turned into aliens in the land of their birth, where millions have been uprooted from their ancestral homes and dumped as if they were rubbish in arid, poverty-stricken Bantustan homelands. I went to one such resettlement camp to which people have been transported, and I've said I'll tell the story of the little girl I met until apartheid is no more.

She came out of the shack where she lived with her widowed mother and sister. I asked her: 'Does your mother get a grant or a pension?'

She said, 'No.'

'What do you do for food?'

'We borrow food.'

You look around the camp and wonder who here would have extra food to lend.

'Have you ever returned any of the food you borrowed?'

'No.'

'What do you do when you can't borrow food?'

'We drink water to fill our stomachs.'

People drink water to fill their stomachs in a land that is a net exporter of food!

Apartheid is in and of itself evil, totally and completely. Apartheid is evil without remainder.

Apartheid cannot be reformed. It has to be destroyed before it destroys our country.

I have no hope of real change from this government unless they are forced. We face a catastrophe in this land, and only the action of the international community by applying pressure can save us. Our children are dying. Our land is burning and bleeding, and so I call upon the international community to apply punitive sanctions against this government to help us establish a new South Africa – non-racial, democratic, participatory and just. This is a non-violent strategy to help us do so.

First explicit call for sanctions, April 1986

The only way to wake up many people in this country, especially white people, is when they are treated as pariahs in the sports world.

Sanctions are meant to be a message. We are not asking people to make decisions based on politics or economics. We are asking you to make a moral decision. Are you on the side of justice or injustice? Are you on the side of humanity or inhumanity? Are you on the side of freedom or oppression? You do something that is right not because other people are going to follow you. You do something that is right because it is right.

You hear so many extraordinary arguments. Sanctions don't work. Sanctions hurt those most of all whom you want to help. That is interesting. I haven't heard similar arguments brought forward in the United States when sanctions are applied at the drop of a hat against Panama, Nicaragua, Libya, Poland. I have to say that I find this new upsurge of altruism from those who suddenly discover they feel sorry for blacks very touching, though it's strange coming from those who have benefited from cheap black labour for many years. Spare us your crocodile tears, for your massive profits have been gained on the basis of black suffering and misery.

If it were possible for the new South Africa, the non-racial democratic South Africa, to come into being without invoking sanctions I would be first to sing hallelujah. But history has still to show us an example of those who, when they have power, are willing to share it voluntarily. So I have consistently supported the imposition of sanctions against the South African government as a non-violent strategy to bring them to the negotiating table, so that they can talk with our authentic representatives about the dismantling of apartheid and a new constitution for a beautiful land. For we have a beautiful land with beautiful people, black and white.

We have a cause that is just. We have a cause that is going to prevail. For goodness' sake, let us not spoil it by the kind of methods that we use. If we do this again, I must tell you that I am going to find it difficult to be able to speak up for our liberation ... It is already difficult in this country to talk the truth, but if we use methods such as the ones that we saw in Duduza, then, my friends, I am going to collect my family and leave a country that I love very deeply, a country that I love passionately ...

Condemning 'necklacings' at East Rand funeral, July 1985

The primary violence in South Africa comes from apartheid, which has acted with brutal and callous efficiency against defenceless people. It detains children, it starves them. It stunts their growth emotionally, physically and intellectually. They suffer from quite preventable deficiency diseases. It tortures and maims its children. It kills children. It sponsors state terrorism through vigilante groups in the black townships, to gloat over so-called black-on-black violence. It has, since 1984, caused the deaths of over 2 000 people, most of these by the government security forces. All this is violence; structural, legalised violence, but violence all the same.

Our people have been peace-loving to a fault. In 1960, protesting peacefully against the pass laws, having campaigned since 1912 non-violently for change in South Africa, 69 of our people were shot in the back as they ran away at Sharpeville. In the ensuing state of emergency, our political organisations, the ANC and the PAC, were banned. They had until then been operating legally and openly and non-violently. They said they had now no option but to undertake the armed struggle.

∼

People who support the *Contras* of Nicaragua and Unita in Angola condemn our freedom fighters as terrorists and call these others freedom fighters. We have never understood the convoluted logic. I have said, and I will say it again, I support the ANC in its goal of a non-racial, democratic and just South Africa, but I do not support its methods. I condemn the violence of apartheid. But I also condemn the violence of those who want to overthrow apartheid. I acknowledge Nelson Mandela as my leader and I am proud to do so. Some call him a terrorist. They called Jomo Kenyatta a terrorist. They called Robert Mugabe a terrorist. They called Samora Machel a terrorist. Today's terrorists have an unconscionable habit of becoming tomorrow's prime ministers and presidents.

Address to the National Press Club, Washington, D.C., 1988

∼

Apartheid is a crime against humanity and a threat to world peace. Apartheid must be destroyed ... The world has tried for 40 years to persuade the South African government gently to end apartheid. The Reagan Administration has tried constructive engagement for over six years. All these efforts have ended in abject and dismal failure. Apartheid remains firmly in place, protected, aided and abetted by the Reagan Administration, by Mrs Thatcher, by Chancellor Kohl. These people are perhaps not racists. Their rhetoric against apartheid is eloquent. But for the victims of apartheid, they are the most effective and the most powerful allies of and collaborators with the vicious, evil, immoral, unchristian, unbiblical policy of apartheid. For apartheid's victims, whether they are in fact racists is of only irrelevant, academic interest. For apartheid's victims, capitalism and free enterprise are the enemies of our people. For as we have experienced them, they have been the most effective partners in our oppression. They are the best recruiters for communism.

We must say to our rulers, especially unjust rulers such as those in this land: 'You may be powerful, indeed, very powerful. But you are not God. You are ordinary mortals! God – the God whom we worship – can't be mocked. Let us say it to you nicely: You have already lost! We are inviting you to come and join the winning side. Come! Come and join the winning side. Your cause is unjust. You are defending what is fundamentally indefensible, because it is evil. It is evil without remainder. It is immoral. It is immoral without question. It is unchristian. Therefore, you will bite the dust! And you will bite the dust comprehensively!'

Let me warn the government yet again as I did when Mr Louis le Grange was Minister of Police, and he made unfounded accusations against the South African Council of Churches: 'Beware when you take on the church of God. Others have tried it before and they came a cropper. They bit the dust and did so ignominiously – the Roman Emperor Nero, Hitler, Amin, and many others. You will end up being part of the flotsam and jetsam of history, hardly a footnote on its pages.'

I told Mr Vlok: 'You know you have lost.' I said it quietly, I didn't shout like now. I said: 'You know you have lost, you know it from your own history. You believed you were being oppressed by the British, you fought against the British and in the end you became free. The lesson you must learn from your own history is that when people decide to be free, nothing, just nothing, absolutely nothing can stop them.'

Reference to the Minister of Law and Order in a 1989 speech

Once I met an anchorite, a person who spends time in solitary prayer. I asked her to tell me about her life and she said, 'Well, I live in the woods in California. My day starts at two in the morning and, Bishop Tutu, I pray for you regularly.' Then I say, 'Hey, here am I being prayed for at two in the morning, in the woods in California. What chance does the South African government stand?'

There were times such as around the 1989 Defiance Campaign when some of our church services were only just religious. When a rally had been banned, we said, okay we'll have a church service to give the people the opportunity to do the things that they would have done in the rally. I am not ashamed we did this because I think if we had not given our people that space, there would have been a great deal more anger to handle in this country.

If the police presence was low-profile, then I'm Bing Crosby.
After a 1989 protest against beach apartheid

At home they tell stories which feature a character called Van der Merwe, who is not over-endowed with intelligence. He was browned off, so they say, because the Americans and the Russians were getting all the praise for their space programmes, so he announced that South Africa was to launch a spacecraft to the sun, no less. Knowledgeable people told him, 'Van der Merwe, it will be burnt to cinders long before it gets anywhere near the sun.' Nothing daunted, Van der Merwe retorted: 'Do you think we South Africans are stupid? We will launch it at night.'

Van der Merwe and his friend Dlangamandla went on holiday to the United States, where they got into big trouble and were convicted of a capital offence. They were given the choice of an electric chair or the rope. Van der Merwe went first and chose the electric chair. He was strapped in and they pulled the switch. Nothing happened. This was repeated three times and they decided to reprieve him. As he went out, Dlangamandla was next in the queue. Van der Merwe told him: 'The damned thing doesn't work. Choose the rope!'

When Steve Biko died in detention, and Jimmy Kruger, the Minister of Police, said, 'It leaves me cold,' we said we were worried for him. What had happened to his humanity, that

45

the death of a fellow human being could leave him cold?

⸻

You don't choose your family. They are God's gift to you, as you are to them. Perhaps if we could, we might have chosen different brothers and sisters. Fortunately or unfortunately, we can't. We have them as they have us, and no matter how your brother may be, you can't renounce him. He may be a murderer or worse, but he remains for ever your brother. Our baptism has made us brothers and sisters. Can you imagine what would happen in this land if we accepted that theological fact about ourselves – that whether we like it or not, we are members of one family? Whether I like it or not, whether he likes it or not, P.W. Botha is my brother and I must desire and pray for the best for him.

⸻

White South Africans are not all horned demons with hidden tails. They are ordinary human beings, most of them scared stiff. But wouldn't you be, if you were outnumbered five to one?

⸻

We sometimes have to say to whites, 'You know, there's a pain that you perhaps can't understand.' I actually once said to some of them, 'You know, we laugh with you but sometimes we laugh only with our teeth.' Because it's been painful for our people. As you go around you say, 'That is where we used to live; it's been broken down and taken over by white people; this is where I used to go to school, it's been demolished, it belongs to white people.' Many of us can tell stories of homes that no longer exist.

The Archbishop of Cape Town has provided sections of the media with someone they could identify as Public Enemy Number One, or at least a very useful scapegoat. But if they have problems with me, they are in real trouble.

Those who accuse Christianity of meddling in politics are almost always the beneficiaries of some status quo or another. You are political almost only when you declare that the status quo is unjust, exploitative and oppressive. For most whites I am a politician trying desperately hard to be a bishop. If this political bishop were to stand up and say, 'Apartheid is not so bad,' then I bet my bottom dollar none of my present critics would call me political. There would be a wonderful metamorphosis.

I had a two-part meeting with the State President. The first was fairly rational. We talked like civilised human beings. Then we changed gears and the temperature dropped several degrees because he came to his point that it was I who was persuading people to break the law. He's fond of becoming, as it were, a heavy-handed, scolding headmaster. I was going to be very subdued, very calm. I could have kept quiet, but I decided I might never get this chance again. Our people had suffered so long. I said, 'One thing you've got to know is that I'm not a small boy. You're not my headmaster.'

But we did get into it like little boys, really. It was a shame, accusations and counter-accusations, that sort of thing. I told him, 'I love this country, probably more than you, because our people fought against the Nazis. You did-n't.' He got very, very angry about that. But it is true – they supported the Nazis.

I don't know whether that's how Jesus would have han-dled it. But at that moment, I didn't quite mind how Jesus would have handled it. I was going to handle it my way. I hope that is how he would have handled it, because it was done on behalf of people who have been hurt by these guys. I thought, he's certainly never heard this from a black per-son in this way. But they've been rough, and they're rough now, to our people.

Description of a meeting with P.W. Botha, 1988

P.W. Botha, in speaking about reforming apartheid instead of destroying it, missed a golden opportunity of ushering in a new dispensation for all South Africans. To turn an English expression around, sadly he lacked the convictions of his courage.

What we are likely to see is just a change in initials. Where you've had a P.W., now you've got an F.W. Really, what has Mr De Klerk shown which would begin to address the problems of this country?

On F.W. de Klerk's rise to power, August 1989

SOUTH AFRICA IN TRANSITION

In August 1989 we were engaged in the Standing for the Truth Campaign in conjunction with the Defiance Campaign. We had decided that apartheid laws did not oblige obedience since they were so grossly unjust and we wanted to help end a vicious and evil system non-violently. We decided in Cape Town to break beach apartheid one Saturday. We had to run the gauntlet of roadblocks manned by heavily armed police, so the people had to face up to police dogs, whips and teargas. At the Strand the police officer in charge warned that if we did not disperse they would use even live ammunition to disperse us. Incredible that they would have shot to kill in order to uphold beach apartheid, to stop God's children from walking on God's beaches.

People died in protests against the racist general election in September. We called on the people of Cape Town, and on 13 September we marched, thirty thousand of us, in a disciplined and impressive demonstration of outrage and to claim the streets of Cape Town for peace. We marched in Cape Town and it fired the imagination and courage of others elsewhere. They began to march in Johannesburg, in East London, in Durban, in Bloemfontein, in large cities and small platteland dorps. It was a demonstration of people power for peace and it must have helped to make 2 February 1990 more possible.

Man, I couldn't believe my ears on 2 February as I listened to Mr De Klerk address parliament and kept pinching myself because I was afraid I might be asleep and would awake to the rude and harsh realities of a rampant apartheid. But I was not dreaming. This man was speaking about what we had been saying should happen in our beautiful country. And even today I want to salute Mr De Klerk for remarkable courage for what he set in motion on that memorable day. Of course he would not have been able to do what he did, had Nelson Mandela been a man consumed by bitterness, hatred and a lust for revenge, had he not been the dignified, almost regal and magnanimous patriot with a passionate love for South Africa and her diverse peoples.

We reacted with emotions nothing short of euphoric when prison doors that had been locked for decades suddenly opened and our leaders emerged and our political organisations, for so long harassed and proscribed, were made legal and could operate aboveboard. We thought the days of teargas, police dogs, whips and bullets were things of the past, which we all wanted to relegate to the pages of history, so that we could set out on the road of reconciliation and negotiations, a road that would lead us to the goal for which so many suffered, for which so many had been detained without trial, for which so many had been imprisoned and exiled and for which so many have died. That goal seemed so close – until all hell was let loose by almost unprecedented violence which put the new South Africa at very considerable risk.

Why has it been so misleadingly called black-on-black
violence? Why don't the media describe the vicious blood-
letting for instance in Northern Ireland as white-on-white
violence? Or that in Eastern Europe? It is also emphatically
not tribal, for in Natal those involved are nearly all Zulus. It
is not Zulu versus Xhosa, for those who live in townships
are people of all tribes who have continued to live together
reasonably harmoniously even at the height of the carnage.

We believe much of the violence is being stoked by a sinis-
ter Third Force, opposed to Mr De Klerk's initiatives, which
wants to see a breakdown of law and order, perhaps paving
the way for a coup against him. He must act firmly against
those in the security forces who want to derail the negotia-
tion process. We believe that there are good soldiers and
good policemen and -women but our country has no culture of tolerance. When someone disagrees with you, then
he is *ipso facto* your enemy and there is only one thing you
do with an enemy – liquidate him. Those who opposed
apartheid have been treated as enemies by the organs of
state. They have been pilloried and vilified by what have
been the state organs of propaganda, SABC-TV and Radio
and other usually sycophantic media. We know now that
people fairly high up in the security establishment ordered
the assassinations of those perceived to be enemies.

The violence is also due to rivalry between political groups
and ideologies. We urge their leaders and adherents to show

the tolerance of maturity. We condemn political violence as the horrible delinquency it is, and we cry out especially against that gruesome way of killing, necklacing. To cajole, compel or intimidate anyone into holding or rejecting a particular point of view is to concede that the point of view cannot persuade acceptance on its own. My father used to say, 'Don't raise your voice – improve your argument!'

If we are confident that we are going to be free, then we ought to be beginning to operate like people who know they are going to be free, who are going to rule themselves. That means we must be disciplined. If you are a soccer team and all of you do what you like, playing to the gallery, you will never score goals. In a good team everybody plays together and you work as a disciplined group.

Our freedom is not absolute but it is enjoyed in community. Consequently, it ideally has community-sanctioned limits which most reasonable individuals will accept since they have a say in their determination. Someone pointed out that your right to stretch your arm ends where my nose begins.

We need a sycophantic press as much as we need a hole in the head.

Conditions are difficult in South Africa with high unemployment and homelessness. Immigrants put pressure on limited resources, and when people look for scapegoats, then almost inevitably the foreigner, the alien, is an easy and ready target. But can we have forgotten so soon that many of our own people were refugees and exiles in the very countries from which the new arrivals come?

❧

I urge our churches to be involved in clean-up campaigns. We live in ghettos, many of us, but we don't have to live like pigs in those ghettos. We are not rubbish, but if we don't get rid of rubbish, then we soon behave as if we were rubbish.

The authorities should impose stiff fines on all those who litter. Singapore is spotlessly clean – they have strict anti-litter laws. In the United States they impose fines as high as $1000 for littering. I suggest a minimum of R100. Perhaps we will realise that littering is a crime as well as a sin. We are spoiling God's creation of which we are meant to be responsible stewards.

❧

God has chosen you Afrikaners for a special role in this land. I used to say that Afrikaners are not subtle. You know where you stand with them. If they said they would put you in your place, then that is what they meant; unlike others who might say the opposite and do as the Afrikaners did.

You are a remarkable people – once you have seen the light, nothing stops you. There are no half-measures with you, you are committed to the hilt. Just see what people like Beyers Naudé, Ben Marais, Dawid Bosch, and others have done, often at great cost to themselves, as they stood up to be counted and were often accused of being traitors.

❧

The greatest handicap Afrikaans has experienced has been

the sense on the part of the deprived and the downtrodden that it was the language of the oppressor. As things change in South Africa and the white does not have to play the role of the one who enjoys putting his boot on the neck of somebody else, there will be no reason to stigmatise Afrikaans or Afrikaners.

❦

I have to say that I don't like what I have seen of capitalism. What I mean is that as a Christian my concern is for the kind of community which is depicted in the Book of Acts, where we are able to share equitably. What does capitalism do? It says we want to encourage what I believe are some of the worst aspects of human nature, that you compete, you see the other person as a rival, as an opponent, somebody to be beaten, you actually use the laws of the jungle. The first Christian community was one that said those who are rich should sell what they have and share. What God would actually want to see, according to the Scriptures, is a community where there are no differences of status.

❦

I believe that an African Marxist–Leninist is a contradiction in terms. Almost all Africans believe in the reality of a spiritual realm. Long before Christianity came, Africans knew there was a supreme being, and their whole way of life is to say that community is made up of those who are physically alive and those, called the ancestors, who are around but are invisible. All Africans take that in with their mother's milk, they can't help it. Therefore an ideology that says to you, The spirit world does not exist, goes totally against the grain. So to be a materialist is virtually impossible. And then to be atheistic, to say there is no God and really believe it, you can do it cerebrally maybe, but I think it's also almost impossible.

⚜

We would say that we understand classical, traditional communism as being materialistic and atheistic. Almost by definition, if it is atheistic, someone who says they believe in God cannot be a member of that particular party. The South African party claims that it is peculiar, that it believes in religious freedom. But our own position is that, taking our stance here *vis-à-vis* classical communism, there is no way in which a Christian can be a member of the Communist Party.

Now that does not mean that we have not co-operated with communists. We co-operate with people of other faiths and people of no faith in striving for certain conditions. In our opposition to injustice we have been ready to accept whoever subscribed to our views as allies. The West had no problems in co-operating with the Russians in fighting Nazism.

⚜

My opposition to communism has got nothing to do with persons. I am very fond of Joe Slovo and I am particularly attracted to Chris Hani. Many black people were treated perhaps for the first time in their lives as human beings by white people who were, almost all of them, communists. It was not communists who oppressed us, it was not communists who thought up apartheid, it was not communists who killed our people in Sharpeville, it was not communists who killed our people in Boipatong. It was Christians who killed us, it was Christians who thought up apartheid, just as it was Christians who were responsible for the Holocaust.

⚬

Elections are usually just secular political events in most parts of the world. Our elections in April 1994 turned out to be a deeply spiritual event, a religious experience, a transfiguration experience, a mountain-top experience. We won't quickly forget the images of those long queues snaking their way slowly into the polling-booths. There was chaos in many places and it should have been a nightmare, but the very fact of arrangements going awry gave us the opportunity of a lifetime. What took place can only be described as a miracle. People stood in those long lines, people of all races in South Africa that had known separation and apartheid for so long, black and white, coloured and Indian, farmer, labourer, educated, unschooled, poor, rich, they stood in those lines and the scales fell off their eyes. South Africans made an earth-shattering discovery: Hey, we are all fellow South Africans. We are compatriots. People shared newspapers, picnic lunches, stories, and they discovered (what a profound discovery!) that they were human together and that they actually seemed to want much the same things – a nice house in a safe neighbour-hood, a steady job, good schools for the children and, yes, skin colour and race were indeed thoroughly irrelevant.

⚬

A black person entered the voting booth and emerged on

the other side a different and transformed person. She entered weighed down by the burden of humiliation, of having had her dignity trodden underfoot, and said, 'Hey, I am free – my dignity, my personhood, have been restored.' A white person burdened by guilt for all the benefits so unjustly enjoyed over the years, entered the booth and emerged on the other side a new, a transformed person, 'Hey, I am free – the weight of guilt has been lifted from my shoulders.' Many white people confessed that they too were voting for the first time as really free people. They realised what we had been trying to tell them for so long, that freedom was indivisible, that they would never be free until we were free.

There were times when you had to whistle in the dark to keep your morale up, and you wanted to whisper in God's ear: 'God, we know you are in charge, but can't you make it a little more obvious.' And now he's done it! It's happened!

We are a sign of hope for the rest of the world. If it could happen here, then there is hope for Rwanda, for Bosnia, for Northern Ireland and peace is coming in the Middle East. If the nightmare of apartheid could end, then all other nightmares everywhere will end. If what used to be regarded as the intractable problem of apartheid could be resolved, then no problem in the world can ever again be considered intractable, insoluble.

RECONCILIATION

We are the Rainbow People! We are the new people of the new South Africa!

Grand Parade, Cape Town, September 1989 march

At home I have sometimes said in big meetings where you have black and white together, 'Raise your hands!' Then I've said, 'Move your hands,' and, 'Look at your hands – different colours representing different people. You are the rainbow people of God.'

The rainbow in the Bible is the sign of peace. The rainbow is the sign of prosperity. We want peace, prosperity and justice, and we can have it when all the people of God, the rainbow people of God, work together.

Tromsö, Norway, 1991

God did not make a mistake in creating us black. We are beautiful. We don't have to shuffle around apologising for our existence. In God's garden there are all kinds of flowers and God did not make a mistake in creating us people of different colours. A rainbow is a rainbow because it has different colours. That is how a rainbow happens. If it had only one colour it would not be a rainbow. We ought to be saying: We are the rainbow people of God because God did not make a mistake in creating us different.

My white brothers and sisters must know that we would want to defend to the death their right to their cultural and racial identities if they want to keep them. We are not looking for a time when we will have a great monotonous uniformity. We want people to remain who they are in the fullness of their individuality, to make their particular, unique contribution to the greater good of this land. The glory of South Africa is in its diversity, a diversity which will make for true unity.

Often there have been those who have wanted to provide a spurious kind of reconciliation, a crying of 'Peace, peace' where there is no peace, a papering over of the cracks instead of dealing with the situation as it demands, seriously facing up to the unpleasantness of it all. In South Africa, we have often heard people speaking disapprovingly of what they have called 'confrontation', which they then opposed to 'reconciliation'.

In this way one of the central features of the gospel of our Lord and Saviour, Jesus Christ, has, as it were, fallen on bad days and been repudiated and looked askance at by those who have had to bear the brunt of apartheid's oppressive injustice and its exploitation. They have been compelled to reject the genuine article because they have been appalled at the counterfeit they have been offered. Glorious gospel words have fallen into disrepute and have been horribly devalued so that many have come to think that 'reconciliation' meant making peace with evil, immorality, injustice, oppression and viciousness, of which they are the victims, and, quite rightly, they have rejected such a travesty of the genuine article.

How could anyone really think that true reconciliation could avoid a proper confrontation? When a husband and wife or two friends have quarrelled, if they merely seek to gloss over their differences or metaphorically paper over the cracks, they must not be surprised that in next to no time, they are at it again, hammer and tongs, perhaps more violently than before because they have tried to heal their ailment lightly. It is a total misreading of the New Testament to think that the picture of our Lord it paints is of the Jesus who is the pale, meek and mild one who could not say 'boo' to a goose. Jesus could throw down the gauntlet to a Herod: 'Go and tell that fox ...' Hardly designed to endear him to that pleasure-loving tyrant. The Jesus who is only meek and mild exists as a caricature.

True reconciliation is based on forgiveness, and forgiveness is based on true confession, and confession is based on penitence, on contrition, on sorrow for what you have done. We know that when a husband and wife have quarrelled, one of them must be ready to say the most difficult words in any language, I'm sorry, and the other must be ready to forgive for there to be a future for their relationship. Equally, confession, forgiveness and reconciliation in the lives of nations are not just airy-fairy religious and spiritual things, nebulous and unrealistic. They are the stuff of practical politics.

Those who forget the past are doomed to repeat it. Just in

terms of human psychology, to have blanket amnesty where no disclosure is made will not deal with our past. It is not dealing with the past to say glibly, Let bygones be bygones, for then they will never be bygones. How can you forgive if you do not know what or whom to forgive?

Even for the perpetrators, an easy and a light cure will not be effective in going into the roots, into the depths of their psyches. It isn't just being Christian, it is actually how human beings operate, when we say that guilt, even unacknowledged guilt, has a negative effect on the guilty. One day it will come out in some form or another. We must be radical. Let us go to the root, remove that which is festering, cleanse and cauterise, and then a new beginning is a possibility.

Forgiveness gives us the capacity to make a new start. That is the power, the rationale, of confession and forgiveness. It is to say, 'I have fallen but I am not going to remain there. Please forgive me.' And forgiveness is the grace by which you enable the other person to get up, and get up with dignity, to begin anew. Not to forgive leads to bitterness and hatred, which gnaw away at the vitals of one's being.

We blacks for our part are ready to forgive, but the other party must be contrite and ready to make reparation to demonstrate the seriousness of their contrition, and then reconciliation can happen. You cannot say you are sorry you stole my pen if you continue to retain possession of it. Your contrition will be demonstrated by your willingness to make amends: in this case, by returning my pen.

We are not looking for a witchhunt, because our country would then have no hope of recovery. But whites have to be ready to say, in respect of the things their white skins have given them: 'To show we are genuinely sorry, we want to give back what we have taken from you.'

—————

The process of confessing and forgiving and making restitution is the kind of thing that would create the atmosphere we need so desperately in this country for beginning to be able to work together, for creating the kind of trust in one another which we need if this country is going to become the great country that God intends it to be.

—————

I want us to see a revival, a renaissance of the wonderful attributes and values of Africa. We have had a jurisprudence, a penology in Africa which was not retributive but restorative. In the traditional setting, when people quarrelled the main intention was not to punish the miscreant but to restore good relations. For Africa is concerned, or has traditionally been concerned, about the wholeness of relationship. That is something we can bring to the world, a world that is polarised, a world that is fragmented, a world that destroys people.

—————

Those who engage in true reconciliation are often caught in the middle, likely to be crushed between those they are trying to reconcile. They may often be reviled and vilified as mealy-mouthed, but they should not be surprised. For

Christians, their paradigm is their Lord, who achieved real reconciliation through an excruciating and shameful death on the Cross. Real reconciliation is costly. It cost God the death of his only son.

Cartoon: Jonathan Shapiro: *Zapiro: The Hole Truth*
(David Philip, 1997)

RENEWAL IN AFRICA

You look round Africa at this time, at God's children suffering all over Africa. The poor are getting poorer, the hungry getting hungrier and all over Africa you see many of God's children suffering oppression. You see God's children often in prison for nothing. All over Africa you see God's children treated as if they were rubbish. Often God's children can't say what they want to say because when they declare, 'This is wrong,' they are taken to prison or killed. Not just in South Africa, although there it is most obvious.

Addis Ababa, 1989

Africa has the unenviable record of producing nearly half of the world's refugees. Some of these are obviously due to natural disasters like flood or drought, but far too many are the victims of human rights violations. Africa's human rights record is horrendous and it makes you feel so deeply saddened that often all that has changed for the so-called ordinary people is the complexion of the oppressor. Whereas formerly under colonial rule the oppressor was someone with a light skin, now for many of God's people the oppressor is someone who has the same skin colour, belongs often to the same ethnic group, often speaks the same language.

We cannot have people say it is bad to have detention without trial in South Africa, and they quite rightly condemn it, and then when it happens elsewhere they expect you to keep quiet. You have to say if it is wrong there, it must be wrong everywhere else where it happens. The thing is wrong whoever perpetrates it.

Khartoum, 1989

Those of us who are engaged in the struggle against apartheid have had considerable inspiration and support from countries in Africa, who have been wonderful, at great cost to themselves, to continue to support us, to receive refugees and exiles from southern Africa. But our struggle against the horrendous policy of apartheid is subverted very considerably by the fact that the perpetrators of apartheid always say, 'Well, look at what they are doing in such-and-such an African country', and they point to far too many of our African countries where the people do not enjoy freedom.

West Africa, 1990

There will be no stability and hence no real lasting prosperity if a land is ruled by those who are corrupt, inefficient, ruthless in their abuse of power, who oppress the poor, who muzzle those who would condemn their excesses, who imprison and torture them and kill; who enrich themselves at the expense of the mass of the people; who maintain themselves in office through the brutal force of an army that does not remain in the barracks but is a repressive instrument to intimidate those it should properly be protecting. Such rulers need an expensive security establishment. They have to travel with a huge entourage in motorcades because they dare not mingle with their sorely tried people. Freedom is much cheaper than repression. In a free society the rulers are popularly chosen and so virtually everyone, except a lunatic fringe, is their bodyguard.

Nairobi, 1994

If the church does not speak out on behalf of the voiceless, who will speak on their behalf?

Cairo, 1989

The church of God must always be vigilant because no matter how popular, no matter how democratic a government is, that government is made up of human beings. They are not God and therefore they are not infallible. The church of God must always be there to say: 'Thus saith the Lord.' The church of God will always be the church that speaks for the hungry, the little ones, the powerless ones, the ones who have no clout.

Zimbabwe, 1991

We must be guardians of the rights of God's children as we strive for justice, equity and goodness, looking for societies that are caring, sharing and compassionate. We must remind rulers that they exist for the sake of the ruled. We should point out that democracy is not just about multi-party elections and parliaments, but more importantly about the participation of the people in the process of making decisions affecting their lives, either directly or through their freely elected representatives. Democracy is also a process in which different and minority views are respected and protected.

―――

We must find ways of making electoral defeat acceptable. People have resented and dreaded going out of office because they were then turned overnight into nonentities after holding prominent positions. We must find ways of governing which are as inclusive as possible. The experiences of Haiti and Lesotho demonstrate how exclusive, majoritarian constitutions almost always lead to trouble and instability and what is happening in South Africa shows that, for example, proportional representation and guarantees to minority groups (at least in transitional periods) contribute to stability and unity when fragmentation and disintegration should have been the consequence.

Kenya, 1994

―――

Once a ruler opens up and says to the people, 'You are free,' the energies released are incredible because people have a pride, a deep patriotism. They want to see their country succeed so they can walk tall, proud, and say, 'I come from Ghana and we are free in Ghana,' or, 'I come from Nigeria and we are free. We can say anything we like.' Africa is too beautiful, too precious, to be left in the hands of dictators.

―――

In Africa people have forgotten the African way of ruling. It is not true that our chiefs were dictatorial. Almost everywhere in Africa the good chief was the person who could listen and then draw a consensus. Consensus happens because people have their different points of view and the good ruler says, 'I have listened to all of you, we are not taking a vote, but listening to you I think most of you are feeling that we must go this way rather than that way.' Now the ruler who could discern what the people wanted was the ruler who lasted on his throne. We would like our rulers to last because they are rulers by the will and consent of the people. We want Africa to be the star of the world because it is a continent that is richly endowed and has been impoverished by rulers who have far too frequently enriched themselves at the cost of the ordinary people.

West Africa, 1990

They tell us to produce, so Africa produces. Then we try to sell what we have produced. We sell to people who dictate the price, then buy it, do a few things to it, then sell it back and decide how much to charge us for what originally came from us.

Africa is burdened by colossal debt, burgeoning largely because it is like playing a soccer match against a team which decides the rules and, after deciding the rules, also has the referee on its side. So even when you succeed in scoring a goal using their rules, they tell you, 'No, you were offside.'

There are countries which do actually produce, which have done a tremendous amount in trying to promote development, and most of what they produce is used to service the debt. The debt doesn't get smaller; all they manage to do is perhaps pay a little bit of the interest.

West Africa, 1990

Now that apartheid has been destroyed, the next item on the world's agenda, the next moral issue that we must pursue, is the foreign debt and the creation of a more equitable economic system.

African and other developing areas need to be given another chance to make a success of what has been called 'the second liberation for reconstruction and development'. Many poor countries are exporting more resources to service their debt than they receive in aid. I am suggesting there should be a six-month moratorium on debt repayments with strict conditions: (a) that the country concerned starts a programme of genuine democratisation, with the people really participating in decision-making; (b) that human rights are promoted and respected; and (c) that the people benefit directly from the money saved.

If these conditions have been met after six months, then the debt should be cancelled. But we must also help to evolve a new economic order so that developing countries are not always at such a disadvantage in matters such as commodity prices. We must press for reforms at the World Bank and the International Monetary Fund so that they become more responsive to the real needs of the people and rethink their policies on issues such as Structural Adjustment Programmes. We need an economic order that acknowledges that people are more important than profits, than things, than possessions. It must be people-friendly.

Kenya, 1994

Westerners are very good at pulling things apart, at breaking them down with their analytical skills. Look at their scientific achievements. But they aren't so good at putting them together. Africa has a gift to the world that the world doesn't have really, the gift of saying that the strict individualism of the West is debilitating. We can't boast about it because it's a gift from God, but the world is going to have to learn the fundamental lesson that we are made for harmony, for interdependence.

The world is discovering we are made for interdependence not just with human beings; we are finding out that we depend on what used to be called inanimate nature. When Africans said, 'Oh, don't treat that tree like that, it feels pain,' others used to say, 'Ah, they're pre-scientific, they're primitive.' It is wonderful now how they are beginning to discover that it is true – that that tree does hurt and if you hurt the tree, in an extraordinary way you hurt yourself. Now they've got long words for these concepts and write PhDs on ecology and so on.

FREEDOM BREAKING OUT

We live in exhilarating, in turbulent and exciting times. We marched first in Cape Town. Then they marched in Europe and the Berlin Wall was breached. Freedom began breaking out in so many and such unlikely places. Tyrants and dictators who had thought themselves so firmly in the saddle began biting the dust ignominiously, as some of us had often predicted in the dark days of naked and blatant repression.

There are moments when we transcend what conspires to divide us, when we reach out to the sublime, to the transcendent, when we seem for a moment to be drawn together as a global family celebrating our humanity, our oneness, our being members of one family. Did we not all thrill at the nobility of the human spirit when that solitary student in Tiananmen Square stood in front of an advancing tank, forcing it to change direction on several occasions? Or when after decades of repression, people formed a human cordon to stop tanks in Manila, so toppling Marcos; or when they did the same as they rallied round Boris Yeltsin and so put paid to the abortive Russian coup?

One of the reasons we are seeing freedom breaking out is that it is an inescapable, inevitable fact of life, whether we like it or not, that this is a moral universe. Right and wrong actually do matter and we cannot engage in conduct that flouts morality and gets away with it for ever. There is a nemesis, and it is that good conduct will ultimately be rewarded. Conversely, wrong conduct will come a cropper. As they say, truth will out no matter how cunningly people may try to cover up. This fact is a great comfort and encouragement for those engaged in apparently unequal struggles with the powers of darkness, which seem to be on the rampage, threatening to carry all before them.

In the bad old days I just had to say we were marching or protesting when our priests would come out in droves. It was enough to rally them to know we were against apartheid. You could say apartheid welded us together. Facetiously one could now ask, 'What are we going to do without apartheid?' It was easy to be against. It is not, it seems, so easy to say what we are for. Although we might say we are for a non-sexist, democratic, non-racial society, there are so many options vying for support in the marketplace that there is a fair degree of confusion and disillusionment. We have even been accused of being without a vision. Who is the enemy out there? Why are things so confusing, and not more straightforward? People are finding it difficult to change from struggle tactics and strategies. The necessary adjustments and changes in mindset have not yet been made.

Whilst we rejoice at the advent of democracy and the privileges and rights that have accrued to us as a result, we should remember that freedom also brings responsibility and obligations and duties. We must get rid of the entitlement culture that only demands. We are no longer able to use apartheid as a convenient scapegoat. Undoubtedly it has left us a horrendous legacy in homelessness, unemployment, poor health care and hopelessly inadequate education. This is now in every sense our country. We are going to make it succeed or fail. We must roll up our sleeves and put our shoulders to the wheel. We must not wait and expect that government will provide. Success depends on all of us doing our bit. President Kennedy said, Don't ask what my country can do for me but what I can do for my country.

Freedom is not licence. Yes, I have rights and I am free to exercise and enjoy them. But in doing so, I must not infringe the rights of others. I have the right to strike, but I do not have the right to take hostages and to harass, intimidate and generally inconvenience other members of the public in exercising my rights. There are standards to be upheld. There are parameters beyond which we should not stray, otherwise we will have anarchy, there will be instability and no one will want to invest in an unstable and chaotic country. Law and order must be maintained, otherwise the dream that is the new South Africa will turn into a horrible nightmare.

Only in 1989 people were being threatened with live ammunition by the police for breaking the apartheid laws. They were ready to kill to maintain an evil and unjust system. Today it would be difficult to find anyone who ever supported apartheid. They are as rare as dinosaurs.

The Bible recognises that we are a mixture of good and bad. We must therefore not be too surprised that most human enterprises are not always wholly good or wholly bad. We should not be surprised at all that those who are today's oppressed could become tomorrow's oppressors. Even a freely elected democratic government is still made up of frail, vulnerable human beings who may or may not succumb to the blandishments of power. We must do all we can to co-operate with the government in the healing, reconstruction and development of southern Africa. But the church must never become this or that party at prayer, however laudable its policies. We must always maintain a critical distance or be in critical solidarity with them. We must not compromise our prophetic independence.

South Africa has most of the world's serious problems writ small. How do First World and Third World, coexisting cheek by jowl, relate to one another? How does affluence relate to stark poverty? How do black and white get to cohere in one community? How do those who are economically developed interact with the underdeveloped or the developing? When we solve our problems the world is going to celebrate because we will have provided others with a paradigm. It is exciting. From having been the world's pariah, we could end up being the model.

God has a dream. It is a dream of a world whose ugliness and squalor and poverty, its war and hostility, its greed and harsh competitiveness, its alienation and disharmony, are changed into their glorious counterparts, when there will be more laughter, joy and peace, where there will be justice and goodness and compassion and love and caring and sharing, when the kingdoms of this world will become as the Kingdom of our God and of his Christ, and he shall reign for ever and ever.

Photo: *Argus*

DESMOND TUTU ON DESMOND TUTU

I suppose it's been one of those wonderful coincidences, if you like, that I am an African with a fairly easy name: Tutu. If I'd had a more outlandish name, it may have been more difficult to get our cause overseas so easily publicised. I think they've got this guy with a big nose and an easy name, and that helped to give people a picture of South Africa.

Your having invited me obviously proves the truth of the adage that distance lands enchantment to the view. You seem oblivious of my all-too-evident warts which those back at home are very quick to spot. This gives rise to some delicious Tutu stories. One of them is about how, when I died, I went to the Pearly Gates. St Peter said, 'No, no. You have to go to the warmer place.' A fortnight later there is frenzied knocking on the doors of heaven. When St Peter goes, he finds the devil himself standing there and asks him, 'Now, what do you want here?' The devil says, 'Well, you sent Bishop Tutu down there, and he's causing so much trouble I have come to ask for political asylum.'

Once, while flying from Durban to Johannesburg and minding my own business as I always do, one of the air hostesses came up to me: 'Excuse me, sir,' she said, 'one of the passengers would like you to autograph a book for them.' I tried to look modest, although I was thinking in my heart that there were some people who recognised a good thing when they saw it. As she handed me the book and I took out my pen, she said: 'You are Bishop Muzorewa, aren't you?'

While preaching in Australia, I suggested to an audience of young people that they should applaud various people. I then asked them to celebrate who they were by clapping themselves. They gave a humdinger of a response. Then I said, 'What about giving God a standing ovation.' Well, they really did their stuff, they nearly took the roof off. Then, without thinking, I said: 'Thank you.'

In the bad old days, when yours truly was the one they most loved to hate, you saw it in the spate of Tutu stories in which I always came to a sticky end. At this time President Reagan decided to come to South Africa to see how his constructive engagement policy was working. As he flew over the Orange River in Air Force One, he saw a sight that warmed the cockles of his heart – for down there were Pik Botha and P.W. in a speedboat, pulling me on water skis. 'Wonderful!' thought the old President. Later he landed and greeted the Bothas effusively. President Reagan said, 'What a tremendous thing – you and Bishop Tutu together like this.' Then he flew off. Pik turned to P.W. and said, 'Nice man, but he doesn't know anything about crocodile hunting.'

Cape Town is famous for its graffiti. Did you see the one that says, 'God loves Boesak and Tutu.' Which is very nice. Until you see at the bottom that somebody else has written: 'The gods must be crazy.'

There used to be graffiti on a wall near our house in Bishopscourt in Cape Town, which said: 'I was an Anglican until I put Tu+Tu together.' Later, when things got better, someone added: 'Yes, but 2+2 = Freedom.'

One advantage of my skin colour is that it doesn't show when I blush.

It would be distinctly odd if instead of saying, 'I am thrilled to be here,' I said 'I am tickled pink.'

When Terry Waite, the Archbishop of Canterbury's assistant, attended my enthronement, a picture was taken of the two of us standing together, and it was published on the front page of a newspaper. Someone claiming to be a friend asked: 'Why were you kneeling?'

Leah and I visited West Point Military Academy in the United States. At the end of the visit the cadets gave me one of their caps as a present. It did not fit me. Someone else would have said the cap was too small, but my wife said: 'Your head is too big.'

Howard University in Washington D.C. wanted to give me a degree, so they asked for my vital statistics to get the right size gown for the graduation ceremony. I said that was easy. Then they asked for the size of my head. I told them that would be more difficult because it changed daily.

One of the Tutu stories tells of how three friends die. Allan Boesak dies and goes to the Pearly Gates. St Peter sends him into a shack and says, 'Allan Boesak, for all your sins, you will occupy this shack with this woman.' And she's one of the ugliest people you could imagine. Then Ted Kennedy comes along and St Peter puts him into his shack, where there is someone even uglier. St Peter says, 'For your sins, Ted Kennedy, you will spend all of eternity with this lady.' Then I come along. St Peter takes me to my shack and waiting there is Brigitte Bardot, no less. And St Peter says, 'For all *your* sins, Brigitte Bardot, you will spend all of eternity with this man.'

I'm getting much too respectable in South Africa. I'm afraid it is largely since I appeared on a TV talkshow to *toyi-toyi* with that extraordinary lady Evita Bezuidenhout.

Cartoon: Jonathan Shapiro: *Zapiro: The Madiba Years*
(David Philip, 1996)